JANUS PRO BY DEEPSEEK

China's AI Model That's Forcing Big Tech to Rethink Everything

How a $6 Million Experiment is Threatening Artificial intelligence Billion-Dollar Giants

Jackson Z. Scott

Table of Contents

Introduction

Artificial intelligence has always been synonymous with power—power to revolutionize industries, reshape economies, and dictate the future of technology. For years, a handful of dominant players controlled this frontier. Companies like OpenAI, Google, Meta, Microsoft, and Amazon poured billions into AI research, racing to build models more powerful, more capable, and ultimately, more indispensable. With limitless funding, cutting-edge hardware, and access to the brightest minds in the world, these tech giants set the rules of the game. The prevailing belief was that only those with deep pockets and vast computational resources could truly lead the AI revolution.

Then came DeepSeek.

Almost out of nowhere, this relatively unknown Chinese AI startup disrupted everything. With the launch of Janus Pro, a multimodal AI model capable of competing with some of the most advanced proprietary models in the world, DeepSeek delivered a message that no one in Silicon Valley expected: AI dominance is not about who spends the most; it's about who innovates the smartest. What made this revelation even more shocking was the cost. While companies like OpenAI reportedly spend billions on their AI models, DeepSeek built Janus Pro for a mere fraction of that—just $6 million. It was a moment that sent ripples through the industry, raising a question that made investors and executives uneasy: Had Big Tech been overpaying all along?

Janus Pro wasn't just another AI model—it was a game-changer. Unlike most AI systems that specialize in either text generation or image creation, Janus Pro combined both in a single, unified framework. It could analyze images with remarkable accuracy, generate realistic visuals, and process complex text-based tasks, all within one architecture. Its performance, according to benchmarks, was competitive with—and in some cases superior to—major players like OpenAI's DALL·E 3, Meta's Emu3-Gen, and Google's top-tier generative AI. But what truly set it apart was something that none of these industry giants had dared to do: it was open-source.

Releasing an AI model of this caliber for free was a bold move, one that went against the entire playbook of proprietary AI development. Instead of locking Janus Pro behind paywalls and exclusive partnerships, DeepSeek made its code and model weights publicly available, inviting developers, researchers, and enthusiasts to experiment, improve, and expand upon its capabilities. In a world where AI innovation had been closely guarded and commercialized by a select few, this decision was revolutionary. It also came with risks. By making Janus Pro open-source, DeepSeek gave others—including competitors—the opportunity to refine and adapt the model, potentially surpassing its original capabilities. But perhaps that was the point. Perhaps DeepSeek wasn't just trying to build a model; it was trying to change the way AI was developed altogether.

The moment Janus Pro hit the scene, the world took notice. In Silicon Valley, where the assumption had always been that AI supremacy required an endless supply of resources, the implications were unsettling. If a Chinese startup could build a model of this caliber with significantly less funding, what did that say about the billion-dollar investments pouring into AI research by Western tech firms? The stock market reacted almost immediately. NVIDIA, a company whose high-performance chips had become the backbone of AI training worldwide, saw its stock take a staggering hit. The mere suggestion that high-end AI development could be done without the most expensive hardware was enough to trigger a major selloff, wiping out billions in market value.

But the shockwaves extended far beyond Wall Street. Governments, particularly in the United

States, had been working to curb China's advancements in artificial intelligence by imposing strict export controls on advanced chips, limiting access to NVIDIA's most powerful hardware. Yet DeepSeek's achievement raised a pressing question: Were these restrictions actually working? If a company like DeepSeek could train an AI model on restricted, lower-end chips and still achieve results comparable to GPT-4, what did that mean for the future of AI competition between China and the West? The geopolitical implications were undeniable.

This book is not just about Janus Pro—it's about what it represents. It's about an AI industry on the brink of transformation, about the shifting balance of power in global technology, and about the realization that the next great leap in artificial intelligence might not come from where we expect. DeepSeek's breakthrough is more than just a headline; it's a signal that the landscape of AI is changing.

Some see Janus Pro as a symbol of progress, proof that innovation is no longer confined to Silicon Valley's walled gardens. Others see it as a threat—a disruption that could shake the foundations of AI investment, challenge Western tech dominance, and redefine the rules of the game. What is certain is that this moment marks the beginning of a new chapter in the AI revolution.

Understanding DeepSeek's rise, the impact of its model, and the forces at play in this unfolding story is crucial for anyone who wants to grasp where AI is headed next. In the chapters that follow, we will unravel how DeepSeek accomplished what seemed impossible, why its success has rattled Big Tech, and what this means for the future of artificial intelligence. This is not just the story of one AI model—it is the story of an industry at a crossroads.

Chapter 1: The Birth of DeepSeek & Its Mysterious Rise

In the world of artificial intelligence, dominance has always belonged to the biggest players—companies with deep pockets, years of research, and direct access to the most powerful computing resources. Every major breakthrough in AI, from language models to image generation, has come from the same handful of tech giants, making it almost impossible for smaller players to compete. Then, almost out of nowhere, a name surfaced that no one had expected: DeepSeek.

Unlike OpenAI, Meta, or Google, DeepSeek had no long history of AI research under its belt. There were no publicized billion-dollar investments, no grand announcements of partnerships with leading tech firms, and no flashy demonstrations of its capabilities ahead of launch. In fact, for most people in the industry, DeepSeek didn't even exist before 2023. And yet, in just a short span of time, it did something no other company had managed to do—it threw Silicon Valley into uncertainty.

DeepSeek was founded in Hangzhou, China, a city that has quietly grown into one of the country's most prominent tech hubs. Known for being home to Alibaba and other rising tech firms, Hangzhou has become a center for cutting-edge research in artificial intelligence. Yet, despite this favorable location, DeepSeek remained largely in the shadows. No major headlines marked its founding, and it didn't have the kind of high-profile executives that usually accompany the launch of an ambitious AI company. It operated under the radar, silently developing technology that would soon disrupt the entire industry.

While major AI firms spent years fine-tuning their models, DeepSeek's approach was different. Instead of spending billions on training the most complex and expensive AI possible, it focused on something far more efficient—finding a way to achieve state-of-the-art results at a fraction of the cost. This decision would prove to be one of the most consequential in AI history.

The company's breakthrough moment came in early 2024, when it announced Janus Pro, a multimodal AI model that claimed to rival some of the best offerings from OpenAI, Meta, and Google. The AI world was skeptical—how could a company that had been practically invisible suddenly release a model that could compete with or even outperform the most advanced AI systems built by the biggest tech giants?

But DeepSeek wasn't just making bold claims. It had the benchmarks to back them up.

Janus Pro reportedly outperformed some of the most respected AI models on key metrics, including image generation, text processing, and multimodal reasoning. Even more astonishing was how it was built: while OpenAI and other major players had spent billions training their latest models,

DeepSeek claimed to have developed Janus Pro for just $6 million.

This revelation alone was enough to send shockwaves through the industry. If an unknown Chinese startup could achieve GPT-4-level performance without the need for unlimited computing resources, what did that mean for the future of AI?

People started to ask questions. Who exactly was behind DeepSeek? Where did its funding come from? How had it developed such an advanced model in complete secrecy? Speculation ran wild. Some believed it was a quiet offshoot of a larger Chinese AI initiative, part of a broader effort to compete with the U.S. in artificial intelligence. Others thought it had simply outmaneuvered the traditional tech giants by developing more cost-effective ways to train AI models.

Whatever the truth, one fact was undeniable: DeepSeek had arrived. And the AI world would never be the same again.

DeepSeek's emergence wasn't just about launching a competitive AI model—it was about challenging the status quo. From the moment it stepped into the spotlight, the company made it clear that it wasn't following the traditional AI playbook set by Silicon Valley. Instead of competing based on who had the most money, the biggest data centers, or the most powerful GPUs, DeepSeek focused on something different: efficiency, accessibility, and a radical rethinking of AI development.

Its mission was bold yet simple—to democratize AI by proving that cutting-edge models didn't have to be locked behind billion-dollar research labs or proprietary corporate control. DeepSeek believed that innovation in artificial intelligence shouldn't be reserved for a handful of elite companies. While OpenAI, Meta, and Google had built their AI empires behind closed doors, DeepSeek saw an opportunity to disrupt the industry by doing the opposite: building powerful AI and making it open-source.

This wasn't just a marketing strategy; it was a direct challenge to the business model that had defined AI for years. The biggest names in AI had turned their models into highly controlled, for-profit products, available only through paywalled APIs and exclusive partnerships. OpenAI, for example, had started as an open-source project but had since transitioned into a closed system, citing concerns over safety and monetization. DeepSeek took the opposite route—releasing its AI for free, allowing developers, researchers, and businesses to access, modify, and build upon it as they saw fit.

Beyond accessibility, DeepSeek's goal was to prove that AI could be developed in a smarter, more cost-effective way. The company sought to challenge the long-standing assumption that massive computing power was the only way to achieve high-performance AI. By demonstrating that a $6 million investment could yield results comparable to billion-dollar projects, DeepSeek wasn't just building a model—it was questioning the very foundation of AI research and development.

At its core, DeepSeek aimed to break the monopoly on AI innovation. The AI industry had been increasingly consolidated into the hands of a few major corporations, each tightly controlling access to their most powerful models. DeepSeek's decision to go open-source wasn't just a technical choice; it was a statement. It sent a clear message that AI should be something everyone can contribute to, refine, and improve upon—not just a privileged few with vast resources.

There was also a strategic element to this approach. By making Janus Pro freely available, DeepSeek harnessed the power of collective intelligence. Instead of relying solely on its in-house team to improve the model, it opened the door for the entire AI community to test, refine, and optimize it. This move had the potential to accelerate progress in ways that closed systems simply couldn't match.

However, there was an unspoken layer to DeepSeek's ambitions—global AI competition. With AI shaping everything from economies to national security, the ability to develop powerful models had become a geopolitical advantage. The United States had placed strict export controls on advanced AI chips, aiming to slow down China's progress in artificial intelligence. Yet, DeepSeek's success in developing Janus Pro—despite using restricted, lower-tier hardware—raised serious questions about the effectiveness of these restrictions. If DeepSeek could achieve GPT-4-like results without access to the most powerful AI chips, what did that mean for the future of AI dominance?

DeepSeek wasn't just another startup trying to make a name for itself. It was a disruptor, an outsider that had entered the AI race with a completely different approach. It wasn't playing by the rules that Silicon Valley had set—it was rewriting them. And in doing so, it had forced the entire industry to reconsider what was possible.

Developing an advanced AI model under normal circumstances requires vast amounts of computing power, an enormous data pipeline, and access to high-end AI chips—most of which are dominated by NVIDIA, the company that supplies almost every major AI player with the specialized processors needed to train deep learning models. However, for a Chinese AI company like DeepSeek, this process was anything but normal.

The United States had long anticipated China's ambitions in artificial intelligence and, as part of a broader technological containment strategy, placed strict export controls on high-performance chips, particularly NVIDIA's A100 and H100 GPUs—the same chips that companies like OpenAI, Google, and Meta used to train their AI models. The idea was simple: restrict access to the best computing hardware and slow down China's AI progress.

Yet, despite these restrictions, DeepSeek managed to develop a model that rivaled GPT-4 and DALL·E 3, seemingly defying the limits imposed by these hardware constraints. This was one of the most surprising aspects of its success—how did it achieve this level of performance without access to the world's most powerful AI chips?

The answer, according to DeepSeek, lay in optimization and efficiency. Unlike traditional AI companies that brute-forced their way to better models by throwing more hardware at the problem, DeepSeek reportedly developed a training strategy that focused on maximizing the potential of less powerful hardware. Instead of using NVIDIA's banned H100 GPUs, DeepSeek trained Janus Pro using H800 chips, which were specifically designed to comply with U.S. export restrictions. While these chips were technically less powerful, DeepSeek's training methods allowed them to be used more effectively, reducing overall computational costs without sacrificing model quality.

But that explanation didn't satisfy everyone. Some experts questioned whether DeepSeek had truly trained Janus Pro using only the hardware it publicly admitted to using. Others speculated that it might have secretly acquired restricted AI chips through unofficial channels or collaborated with other Chinese research groups that had access to alternative computing infrastructure. While there was no concrete evidence to support these theories, the skepticism itself underscored just how unexpected DeepSeek's breakthrough had been.

Even more mystery surrounded DeepSeek's funding and possible government ties. Unlike OpenAI, which had publicly disclosed its multi-billion-dollar partnerships with Microsoft, or Meta, which had an established history of investing heavily in AI, DeepSeek's financial backing was unclear. Where had it secured the resources to develop such an advanced model in such a short period?

One possibility was that private investors in China saw the strategic value of funding an AI project capable of rivaling Silicon Valley's biggest names. China had already made AI development a national priority, and several large tech firms—including Baidu, Alibaba, and Tencent—had actively invested in AI research. However, none of these companies had publicly claimed involvement with DeepSeek, making it unlikely that a major corporation was secretly behind its rise.

The other, more controversial theory was that DeepSeek had received quiet backing from the Chinese government. AI had become a crucial battlefield in the global tech race, and China had been pushing aggressively to develop domestic alternatives to Western AI technologies. Some analysts speculated that DeepSeek's ability to develop a high-performing AI model so quickly—despite limited resources—hinted at undisclosed state support. If true, this would mean that DeepSeek wasn't just another startup—it was part of a much larger national AI strategy aimed at bypassing U.S. restrictions.

What fueled these suspicions further was the way DeepSeek's AI assistant handled politically sensitive topics. Some users reported that Janus Pro refused to answer questions about the Chinese government or President Xi Jinping, reinforcing the idea that DeepSeek's AI was being closely monitored or influenced by Chinese authorities. While this wasn't definitive proof of government involvement, it certainly raised questions about how truly independent DeepSeek was.

Despite these speculations, DeepSeek remained largely silent about its funding sources and potential political connections. Unlike OpenAI or Anthropic, which regularly engaged with the media and discussed their funding rounds, DeepSeek operated in relative secrecy. It didn't seek widespread publicity before its launch, it didn't host major conferences or research presentations, and it didn't aggressively market itself like most AI companies trying to gain traction.

This lack of transparency only deepened the intrigue. Was DeepSeek a clever underdog that had outsmarted Big Tech? Or was it part of a larger, more coordinated effort to shift the balance of AI power away from the United States?

Whatever the truth, one thing was clear—DeepSeek had proven that U.S. chip restrictions weren't enough to stop China's AI progress. And if it could do it once, there was nothing stopping others from following in its footsteps.

Chapter 2: Enter Janus Pro – The Model That Shook the Industry

Janus Pro wasn't just another AI model—it was a direct challenge to the most powerful artificial intelligence systems in the world. At a time when AI was becoming increasingly specialized, with different models excelling in specific domains—some designed purely for text, others for image generation, and a few experimenting with multimodal capabilities—DeepSeek took a bold step in a different direction. It built an AI system capable of handling multiple types of tasks at once, from text generation to image analysis and even high-quality visual synthesis.

Multimodal AI was nothing new, but achieving it at a competitive level was something only a few companies had managed to do successfully. OpenAI's GPT-4, for example, introduced GPT-4V (Vision), which allowed it to analyze images in addition to generating text. Meanwhile, OpenAI's DALL·E 3 focused purely on image generation, while Meta's Emu3-Gen and Google's AI projects explored similar territory. These models were built by companies with billions in funding, massive computing resources, and access to state-of-the-art AI chips.

Yet here was Janus Pro—a model built on a fraction of the budget—delivering results that competed with, and in some areas outperformed, these AI giants.

What made Janus Pro stand out was its unified Transformer architecture, a design that allowed it to seamlessly handle text-based tasks, image analysis, and image generation within a single model. This differed from many other AI models that relied on separate networks or fine-tuned variations for each function. In other words, rather than needing different AI models for different tasks, Janus Pro combined all of these capabilities into one highly efficient system.

In terms of image generation, comparisons between Janus Pro and DALL·E 3 or Stable Diffusion XL (SDXL) revealed some interesting trade-offs. Janus Pro was capable of faithfully following text prompts, sometimes even better than SDXL, which had a tendency to prioritize artistic quality over strict adherence to the request. However, when it came to image sharpness and artistic detail, DALL·E 3 and SDXL still had an edge. Users who tested the models found that while Janus Pro was surprisingly good at capturing requested details, its outputs sometimes lacked the refined crispness and aesthetic appeal of specialized image-generation models.

When compared to GPT-4V (Vision) in image understanding, Janus Pro performed well on object detection and basic relationships between objects. It could analyze an image and describe its contents accurately, making it useful for computer vision tasks. However, when the task required deeper reasoning or interpreting symbolic meaning, it sometimes fell short. For example, if given an artistic illustration with hidden metaphors, Janus Pro would describe the literal elements in the image but struggle to explain the underlying concept or message, whereas GPT-4V was more capable of grasping symbolic interpretations.

Despite these minor shortcomings, Janus Pro's biggest strength lay in its versatility. Instead of being locked into one function, it could adapt across different types of AI tasks, making it one of the most flexible and accessible AI models available to the public. And unlike OpenAI's proprietary models, which required API access and were hidden behind paywalls, Janus Pro was open-source, meaning developers worldwide could modify, fine-tune, and improve it.

The open-source nature of Janus Pro also meant that it had the potential to evolve at a much faster rate than its closed-source competitors. While OpenAI and Google had control over their models and dictated how they were used, Janus Pro could be experimented on, optimized, and extended by independent researchers and AI enthusiasts around the world. This posed an entirely new kind of challenge for Big Tech: Could a model that was built for free use by the global AI community actually outpace models developed with billions in funding?

It was a question that made Silicon Valley uneasy.

When Janus Pro entered the AI scene, the industry was caught off guard. It wasn't just another AI model—it was a challenge to everything people thought they knew about AI development. For years, the assumption had been that the most powerful AI systems could only be built by companies with billions in funding, thousands of high-end GPUs, and access to exclusive datasets. Yet, here was a model that claimed to match or even surpass some of the biggest names in AI, all while being developed with a budget that was a fraction of what major tech firms were spending. The only way to validate such bold claims was through hard data and rigorous benchmarking.

DeepSeek knew this, and instead of relying on marketing hype, it provided numbers. Janus Pro was tested against some of the most well-known AI models in the industry, including OpenAI's GPT-4V and DALL·E 3, Meta's Emu3-Gen, and Stable Diffusion XL (SDXL). It was put through some of the toughest multimodal AI benchmarks, which evaluated its ability to generate images, analyze visual content, and understand complex relationships between text and imagery. The results were surprising even to those who had initially dismissed the model as just another open-source experiment.

One of the most telling benchmarks was GenEval, a widely respected test that measures how well AI models handle multimodal reasoning. This benchmark assesses an AI's ability to not just describe what's in an image, but also understand the context, relationships, and implied meanings. Janus Pro outperformed OpenAI's DALL·E 3 and Meta's Emu3-Gen on GenEval scores, proving that it wasn't just a competent model—it was a serious contender.

The DPG Benchmark, another industry-standard evaluation, further validated Janus Pro's capabilities. This benchmark focused on how accurately AI models could generate images from textual descriptions and whether they could capture fine details while maintaining logical coherence. Where other models occasionally missed key elements in their image generations or produced overly stylized interpretations, Janus Pro consistently aligned its output with the exact specifications given in prompts. This was a crucial win—especially against models like SDXL, which, while visually stunning, sometimes prioritized artistic expression over strict adherence to the input.

Real-world tests by AI enthusiasts and researchers provided even more insight. When users prompted different models to generate the same image, the results highlighted clear distinctions in performance. A simple request such as "A baby fox curled up under an orange maple tree in autumn, with golden sunlight filtering through the leaves" became a litmus test for accuracy. While SDXL and DALL·E 3 both produced aesthetic and visually impressive images, they often took creative liberties—sometimes making the fox appear too mature, adding extra elements that weren't requested, or adjusting the lighting in ways that deviated from the prompt.

Janus Pro, on the other hand, displayed a remarkable ability to stay true to the description. The baby fox actually looked like a baby, the maple tree was accurately colored in autumn hues, and the sunlight was positioned exactly as described. While its image sharpness wasn't always as refined as DALL·E 3's, its ability to follow instructions with precision made it stand out. This level of prompt adherence was one of its strongest advantages, making it a valuable tool for users who required detailed, instruction-specific outputs.

But image generation was only part of the equation. Janus Pro also went head-to-head with GPT-4V (Vision) in image analysis and reasoning tasks. This included its ability to describe complex images, identify objects, and interpret relationships between elements. In straightforward tasks, such as identifying objects in a photograph or explaining the physical positioning of items, Janus Pro performed at a near-identical level to GPT-4V. It correctly described images, labeled objects, and made accurate spatial assessments.

However, when tasked with abstract reasoning, the difference between the two models became apparent. If given an allegorical painting or an artistic representation of a social issue, GPT-4V had a stronger ability to analyze hidden meanings and symbolism. Janus Pro would give an accurate literal description of the painting—identifying colors, objects, and basic themes—but struggled to explain deeper metaphorical significance.

This highlighted an important distinction: Janus Pro excelled in raw accuracy, but when it came to nuanced interpretation, OpenAI's model had a slight edge. Still, for many real-world applications—such as medical imaging, security analysis, or manufacturing AI—accuracy mattered more than metaphorical reasoning, making Janus Pro a powerful alternative for practical use cases.

One of the most staggering revelations from these benchmarks was the cost-to-performance ratio. OpenAI and Meta had invested hundreds of millions, even billions, in training their latest AI models, leveraging some of the most powerful computing infrastructure available. DeepSeek, by contrast, had trained Janus Pro for just $6 million, using less powerful NVIDIA H800 chips rather than the banned H100 GPUs that Western companies relied on.

This begged an uncomfortable question for Silicon Valley: Was Big Tech overpaying for AI development?

If Janus Pro could achieve similar or even superior results using far less computing power, it meant that efficient training strategies might be more important than sheer processing power. The idea that AI dominance was exclusively tied to who had the most high-end chips and the biggest supercomputers was suddenly in doubt.

Investors took notice. The financial markets reacted sharply, with NVIDIA's stock taking a massive hit, losing over $600 billion in value in a single day. The drop reflected a new concern—if AI companies no longer needed the most expensive NVIDIA chips to compete, then the entire AI hardware market might not be as indispensable as once thought.

This wasn't just an isolated event; it was a signal that the rules of AI development were changing. Instead of an arms race for more GPUs, bigger datasets, and unlimited cloud resources, DeepSeek had shown that innovation in AI was no longer about who had the most—it was about who used it the smartest.

What Janus Pro had done wasn't just about outperforming benchmarks; it was about proving that AI could be built differently. It had exposed a major flaw in how the AI industry had been operating—one that Big Tech could no longer ignore.

Janus Pro's impact on the AI world wasn't just about performance—it was about how it was built. Unlike many of its competitors, which relied on separate networks for different tasks, DeepSeek took a different approach, designing an AI model that was unified and highly efficient. At the core of this breakthrough was its Unified Transformer Architecture, a structural advancement that allowed it to handle text, images, and multimodal tasks within a single system.

Traditional AI models often specialize in either language generation or image processing, requiring separate architectures that were fine-tuned for their specific domains. OpenAI, for instance, used distinct models for GPT-4V (for vision) and DALL·E

3 (for image generation), while Stable Diffusion's image models were trained with a different approach entirely. This meant that even when multimodal capabilities were introduced, they often involved integrating separate models rather than developing a truly unified framework.

DeepSeek bypassed these inefficiencies by designing Janus Pro to function seamlessly across multiple domains. With the Unified Transformer Architecture, a single model could understand, interpret, and generate both text and images without needing distinct subsystems. This not only reduced the computational cost of training but also improved the model's ability to merge different types of information. For instance, when analyzing an image and generating a description, Janus Pro could draw upon its text-based reasoning capabilities in real-time, rather than relying on an external language model to process its findings.

The efficiency of this design was one of the key reasons why Janus Pro was able to match the performance of billion-dollar AI projects despite being trained on lower-tier hardware. By minimizing redundancies and ensuring that different forms of data could be processed within a single framework, DeepSeek was able to achieve more with less, proving that raw computing power wasn't the only way to push AI forward.

But perhaps the most radical move DeepSeek made wasn't in the model's architecture—it was in the decision to release it for free. In an industry where AI breakthroughs were increasingly being locked behind corporate paywalls, DeepSeek did something almost unheard of: it made Janus Pro open-source.

This decision was a direct challenge to the closed ecosystems that had come to dominate the AI landscape. OpenAI, despite its name, had transitioned away from an open-source model, restricting access to its most powerful AI tools. Google and Meta had followed similar paths, keeping their best models behind API-based access, limiting who could use them and for what purposes. The justification for this was often framed as a concern for AI safety and responsible use, but many critics saw it as a strategy to maintain control over the AI industry.

DeepSeek's approach flipped that model on its head. Instead of restricting access, it published the model's weights and code, making it available for developers, researchers, and AI enthusiasts around the world. This wasn't just about transparency—it was a deliberate push to democratize AI.

The implications of this move were massive. By allowing the global AI community to study, refine, and modify Janus Pro, DeepSeek effectively outsourced its model's improvement to thousands of independent researchers. Where companies like OpenAI had to spend billions in R&D to continuously improve their models, DeepSeek's open-source approach meant that Janus Pro's capabilities could evolve organically, shaped by contributions from developers worldwide.

This also raised a fundamental question about the future of AI development. If open-source models like Janus Pro could be fine-tuned and optimized by independent teams, would they eventually outpace closed-source models that relied on centralized corporate research? The rapid evolution of open-source AI had already proven its power—projects like Stable Diffusion had demonstrated how community-driven models could rival and even surpass corporate-backed competitors.

But the decision to go open-source came with risks as well. By releasing Janus Pro to the public, DeepSeek had no control over how it would be used, modified, or repurposed. While open-source AI could lead to groundbreaking advancements, it could also make it easier for bad actors to develop unregulated versions of the technology, raising concerns about misinformation, deepfakes, and ethical misuse.

Still, DeepSeek had made its stance clear. It believed that the benefits of open AI outweighed the risks, and that restricting access to powerful AI tools only served to entrench the dominance of a few major corporations. Whether this decision would ultimately help or hurt Janus Pro in the long run remained to be seen, but one thing was undeniable—it had forced the industry to rethink the way AI should be built, shared, and developed.

Chapter 3: The $6 Million Disruption – Breaking AI's Billion-Dollar Monopoly

When DeepSeek announced that it had developed Janus Pro for just six million dollars, the claim seemed almost too good to be true. For years, the dominant belief in AI development was that creating a powerful model required vast financial and computational resources. Companies like OpenAI, Google, and Meta were spending hundreds of millions, even billions, on training their most advanced AI systems, building massive data centers, and securing access to the most powerful NVIDIA chips available. Yet here was a relatively unknown startup from China, claiming it had built a model capable of competing with some of the best in the industry—at a cost that was just a fraction of what the big players were investing.

The natural reaction from many in the AI world was skepticism. How could DeepSeek have achieved this without cutting corners? Was it simply exaggerating its numbers, or had it discovered a more efficient way to train AI?

The answer lay in a fundamentally different approach to AI training. Instead of following the traditional brute-force method, where models are trained using as much computational power as possible, DeepSeek focused on making the process smarter, not bigger. It optimized everything, from how the data was processed to the way the model learned over time.

One of the biggest cost-saving measures was the use of NVIDIA's H800 chips instead of the high-end H100 GPUs used by companies like OpenAI and Google. Due to U.S. export restrictions, Chinese companies were blocked from purchasing the latest and most powerful AI chips. But instead of this being a setback, DeepSeek turned it into an advantage. The H800 chips were less powerful than the H100, but by refining how they were used in training, DeepSeek managed to achieve near-equivalent results without the need for excessive computing power.

A major factor in AI training costs is energy consumption. Training large models requires running high-performance GPUs for extended periods, sometimes for months at a time. OpenAI, for example, had reportedly spent hundreds of millions of dollars just on cloud computing resources to train GPT-4. DeepSeek, on the other hand, reduced energy costs through a more efficient training pipeline, ensuring that computational resources were used only when absolutely necessary.

Another key advantage was DeepSeek's ability to leverage open-source models and frameworks. While companies like OpenAI and Google built their models almost entirely from scratch, DeepSeek benefited from existing research and innovations in the AI space. It borrowed from and improved upon publicly available algorithms and architectures, allowing it to skip over some of the most expensive early stages of AI development.

In particular, DeepSeek took inspiration from models like Meta's LLaMA, which had proven that smaller, highly optimized models could achieve near-state-of-the-art performance. By using techniques such as selective fine-tuning and data-efficient training, DeepSeek ensured that Janus Pro learned only from the most relevant and high-quality data, reducing the need for costly large-scale training runs.

Beyond technical optimizations, DeepSeek's leaner development structure also played a role. Unlike OpenAI and Google, which employed thousands of researchers, DeepSeek operated with a smaller, more focused team. This meant that it could move faster, experiment with new approaches without bureaucratic delays, and allocate resources more efficiently.

The difference in AI development costs between DeepSeek and Big Tech was staggering. OpenAI, with its deep partnership with Microsoft, had spent billions on building data centers to house the massive clusters of GPUs needed for training. Google had similar infrastructure in place, with custom-built AI supercomputers dedicated to its models. Meta, too, had been pouring resources into AI, investing heavily in research, training, and deployment.

DeepSeek's six-million-dollar experiment shattered the notion that AI breakthroughs were reserved for the companies with the deepest pockets. If a company with far fewer resources could develop a model that was competitive with some of the most advanced AI systems in the world, it meant that the industry's approach to AI development was fundamentally flawed.

The revelation sent shockwaves through the AI sector. Investors began questioning whether AI companies were over-investing in infrastructure, burning money on unnecessary computing power, and following outdated training strategies. Some began to wonder whether AI research had been trapped in a cycle of excessive spending, where companies assumed that throwing more resources at a problem was the only way to stay ahead.

DeepSeek had exposed a simple but profound truth—AI innovation was not just about having the biggest budget, but about making the smartest choices. And for the first time, Big Tech had to face the possibility that a small, agile startup had found a way to outmaneuver them using intelligence, efficiency, and a completely different mindset.

The AI industry has long been dominated by a handful of powerful companies, each racing to build the most advanced models at any cost. OpenAI, Google, and Meta have poured billions into AI research and development, with massive budgets dedicated to training, infrastructure, and deployment. The sheer scale of their spending has reinforced the belief that only the wealthiest corporations with access to unlimited computing power can lead the AI revolution. Then came DeepSeek, a relatively unknown startup from China, which claimed to have developed a multimodal AI model that could compete with these giants—all on a budget of just six million dollars. The contrast was staggering, and it raised a crucial question: why were these big tech companies spending so much while DeepSeek was able to do it for a fraction of the cost?

The answer lay in the fundamental differences in approach. OpenAI, Google, and Meta have positioned themselves as industry leaders, meaning their AI development isn't just about performance—it's about dominance. Their models are designed to serve millions, if not billions, of users, requiring them to build enormous data centers, optimize for large-scale deployment, and ensure that their models can handle vast amounts of traffic without failure. These companies don't just create AI—they create commercial AI products that are deeply integrated into search engines, cloud services, advertising platforms, and enterprise solutions. This level of scalability demands enormous investments in computing power, server maintenance, and security.

DeepSeek, on the other hand, didn't have the same priorities. Rather than optimizing for massive user bases or enterprise-level integration, its primary goal was to prove that high-performance AI could be developed efficiently and affordably. This allowed the company to focus solely on model development, rather than the massive operational costs associated with global AI deployment. OpenAI, for example, has to invest heavily in cloud infrastructure because ChatGPT serves millions of users daily, requiring massive GPU clusters to run inference in real-time. DeepSeek didn't have to worry about this because its model was released as an open-source project, leaving the burden of scaling up to the AI community rather than handling it internally.

Another major factor was the difference in training strategies. Companies like OpenAI and Google take a brute-force approach to AI training, throwing massive amounts of computing power at their models to squeeze out every possible performance gain. The belief has always been that the more data and compute you have, the better the model will be. This philosophy has led to billion-dollar investments in AI training, with companies running multiple training cycles over months or even years to refine their models.

DeepSeek, on the other hand, took a cost-conscious approach. Instead of relying on the most powerful AI chips available, it used NVIDIA's H800 GPUs, which are less powerful than the H100 chips that Western tech companies use for AI training. Rather than letting this hardware limitation hold them back, DeepSeek developed optimized training techniques that allowed Janus Pro to learn more efficiently, reducing the number of computational cycles needed to achieve high performance. This efficiency-first mindset meant that the company didn't need to rent or build massive cloud computing infrastructure, significantly lowering costs.

Another area where DeepSeek saved money was in its reliance on open-source research. OpenAI, Google, and Meta all conduct extensive in-house research, requiring them to fund entire teams of top-tier AI scientists, engineers, and data scientists who push the boundaries of AI innovation. These companies build proprietary architectures, train models from scratch, and conduct long-term experiments that drive up development costs. DeepSeek, on the other hand, took a more pragmatic route, leveraging existing research, adopting techniques from open-source AI models, and refining them rather than reinventing the wheel. This strategy allowed the company to move quickly without having to fund large-scale foundational research.

Big tech companies also have to consider business interests when developing AI, which adds another layer of expenses. For instance, OpenAI has deep financial ties with Microsoft, which means its models are optimized to work within Microsoft's cloud ecosystem, requiring additional engineering resources to ensure smooth integration. Similarly, Google and Meta's AI development is closely tied to their advertising, search, and social media businesses, which means that their models are trained and fine-tuned for highly specific use cases. DeepSeek, on the other hand, wasn't trying to fit its AI into an existing corporate infrastructure, allowing it to avoid many of the costly customizations and optimizations that big tech companies have to consider.

Perhaps the biggest reason DeepSeek's AI development was so much cheaper is that it had no need to commercialize its model. OpenAI, Google, and Meta have to build AI systems that generate revenue, which means they need to invest in product development, marketing, security, and user experience. OpenAI, for example, spends millions ensuring that its AI-powered products are user-friendly, reliable, and monetizable. DeepSeek had no such concerns. By open-sourcing Janus Pro, it eliminated the costs associated with productization, instead allowing the AI community to take the model and build upon it as they saw fit.

The six-million-dollar price tag of Janus Pro wasn't just a reflection of smart engineering—it was a statement about how bloated and inefficient AI development had become in the hands of big tech. DeepSeek proved that AI breakthroughs weren't reserved for billion-dollar companies and that a leaner, more strategic approach could yield results that were just as impressive. The revelation that AI could be developed efficiently sent shockwaves through the industry, forcing companies to rethink their spending strategies. If DeepSeek could achieve state-of-the-art results on a fraction of the budget, what did that say about the way AI research had been conducted all along?

This wasn't just a victory for DeepSeek—it was a wake-up call for the entire AI industry. The assumption that progress in AI required ever-growing budgets was now in question, and for the first time, big tech had to face the uncomfortable reality that a small, agile company had found a way to compete without spending billions.

DeepSeek's ability to train Janus Pro with a budget of just six million dollars was not the result of luck or shortcuts—it was a direct consequence of strategic decisions in training methodology and efficiency-focused development. In an industry where AI models are usually built by throwing massive amounts of computing power at the problem, DeepSeek took a different approach, proving that intelligence and optimization could replace brute force. This not only allowed it to develop a high-performance AI model at a fraction of the usual cost, but it also posed a direct challenge to the dominant AI development strategies used by OpenAI, Google, and Meta.

One of the key factors behind DeepSeek's efficiency was its approach to dataset selection. Unlike major AI labs that train models on massive, unfiltered datasets—sometimes in the trillions of words—DeepSeek adopted a more refined strategy. Rather than training Janus Pro on every piece of available internet data, it focused on smaller, high-quality datasets that were carefully curated for accuracy, relevance, and informativeness. This significantly reduced the amount of computing power required while ensuring that the model learned from cleaner, more reliable data. By eliminating unnecessary noise from training data, DeepSeek allowed Janus Pro to achieve strong generalization without wasting resources on irrelevant or low-quality information.

Another crucial innovation was DeepSeek's method of training optimization. Many Western AI companies rely on redundant training cycles, where they retrain models multiple times on massive datasets to refine performance. This process is computationally expensive, requiring thousands of high-performance GPUs running for extended periods. DeepSeek, on the other hand, leveraged more efficient fine-tuning techniques that allowed Janus Pro to reach high accuracy in fewer iterations. Instead of retraining the entire model from scratch every time an update was needed, DeepSeek applied targeted training improvements, reducing computational waste while maintaining performance gains.

In addition, DeepSeek employed dynamic learning rate scheduling and adaptive computation, techniques designed to reduce unnecessary training steps. By allowing the model to focus on the most complex and informative data samples rather than processing all data equally, Janus Pro was able to improve faster while using fewer resources. This stands in contrast to the traditional Western approach, where models are often trained for longer than necessary in pursuit of marginal improvements.

Hardware constraints also played a role in DeepSeek's innovative approach. Due to U.S. restrictions on AI chip exports, DeepSeek had to train Janus Pro using NVIDIA's H800 chips instead of the cutting-edge H100 GPUs that OpenAI and Google used. Rather than seeing this as a limitation, DeepSeek developed novel ways to maximize the efficiency of its available hardware. By using parallel processing strategies, model quantization techniques, and weight-sharing optimizations, it was able to extract more performance from less powerful chips. This allowed it to achieve results that would have typically required high-end GPUs, proving that AI training could be optimized in ways that Western companies had largely overlooked.

The implications of these techniques extend far beyond DeepSeek itself. For years, the dominant AI development model in the West has been based on the idea that bigger is always better—bigger datasets, bigger compute clusters, and bigger budgets. OpenAI, for example, has partnered with Microsoft to build massive supercomputers for AI training, investing billions into infrastructure to maintain an edge. Google has taken a similar path, integrating its AI efforts with its cloud business to leverage vast amounts of computing power. These companies have been so focused on scaling up that they have rarely stopped to question whether their approach is the most efficient one.

DeepSeek's success presents a direct challenge to this mindset. If a small company with a fraction of the budget can produce an AI model that competes with GPT-4-level systems, then what does that say about the necessity of billion-dollar AI investments? It raises a critical question: has Western AI development become trapped in a cycle of over-engineering and wasteful spending? If efficiency-focused approaches like DeepSeek's prove to be scalable, it could force a complete reevaluation of how AI research is conducted.

This shift is already beginning to affect the way investors and companies think about AI. When it was revealed that DeepSeek had achieved its breakthrough on such a low budget, the stock market reacted immediately. NVIDIA, which had been riding a wave of massive AI investment, saw a sharp decline in value as investors began to worry that the demand for high-end GPUs might not be as unstoppable as previously believed. The broader AI industry also started questioning whether its infrastructure-heavy approach was sustainable.

Beyond the financial impact, there is also a geopolitical dimension to this challenge. The U.S. has relied on export controls to limit China's AI progress by restricting access to advanced chips, assuming that without cutting-edge hardware, Chinese AI companies would fall behind. DeepSeek's success proves that this assumption may be flawed. If efficiency-focused training techniques can produce models that rival those trained on top-tier hardware, then the entire strategy of AI containment comes into question.

Western AI leaders now face a difficult choice. They can either continue investing in massive, expensive infrastructure in the hope that scale will always give them an edge, or they can rethink their approach, adopting some of the techniques that allowed DeepSeek to achieve its results so efficiently. Either way, one thing is clear: AI research is no longer just a game of who can spend the most. DeepSeek has shown that smarter, leaner AI development is not only possible but potentially more effective than the brute-force strategies that have dominated the field until now.

Chapter 4: The AI Stock Market Shock & Big Tech's Response

The financial world has always been deeply intertwined with the progress of artificial intelligence, and nowhere was this clearer than in the meteoric rise of companies like NVIDIA, which became the backbone of AI development. For years, investors poured billions into AI chip manufacturers, believing that the demand for high-performance computing would only continue to grow. AI companies like OpenAI, Google, and Meta needed access to the most advanced GPUs, leading to an arms race in chip production. NVIDIA's dominance in the industry seemed unstoppable, with its stock price soaring as AI adoption accelerated. But then DeepSeek entered the picture, and suddenly, everything changed.

When news broke that DeepSeek had developed a GPT-4-level AI model for just six million dollars—using restricted, less powerful H800 chips rather than NVIDIA's top-tier H100 hardware—investors panicked. If a Chinese startup with limited access to cutting-edge GPUs could achieve such high performance, it meant that AI development might not be as reliant on NVIDIA's most expensive chips as previously thought. The revelation sent shockwaves through the stock market, triggering a massive selloff of NVIDIA shares.

In a single day, NVIDIA's market valuation dropped by an astonishing six hundred billion dollars. The AI boom had largely been built on the assumption that every major tech company would need to purchase thousands, if not tens of thousands, of high-end GPUs to remain competitive. But DeepSeek's efficiency-focused approach raised serious doubts about whether these massive investments in AI hardware were truly necessary. If AI models could be trained using cheaper, less power-intensive chips, then the demand for top-tier GPUs could decline significantly, undermining the very foundation of NVIDIA's dominance.

The ripple effects of this stock market plunge extended beyond NVIDIA. Investors who had been bullish on AI hardware companies began reconsidering their positions, fearing that the industry had overestimated the importance of raw computing power. AI chip manufacturers, data center providers, and cloud computing firms all saw their stocks take a hit as questions emerged about the long-term sustainability of their business models. If AI breakthroughs could be achieved through smarter software techniques rather than brute-force hardware scaling, then many of the companies betting on an AI-fueled demand surge for GPUs and supercomputing infrastructure might need to rethink their strategies.

The drop in NVIDIA's stock price wasn't just about DeepSeek itself—it was about the broader implications of what this breakthrough represented. For years, AI development had been built on the assumption that progress required ever-larger computational resources. The companies leading the industry had operated under the belief that their ability to acquire the best GPUs and build the largest training clusters would always give them an advantage. DeepSeek shattered this belief overnight.

The market reaction reflected a deeper uncertainty about where AI was headed. If a company could develop a competitive model using optimized training techniques rather than relying on sheer compute power, it opened the door for a wave of smaller, more agile AI startups to challenge the dominance of big tech firms. Investors who had previously assumed that AI research was a game exclusively for the wealthiest companies were now forced to reconsider.

The implications for the AI chip market were profound. If efficiency-focused AI development became the new standard, it could fundamentally alter the demand for high-end GPUs. Companies that had been stockpiling NVIDIA chips, assuming they were the key to staying ahead in AI, might suddenly find themselves sitting on hardware that was no longer as essential as they once thought. This could lead to a shift in investment strategies, with a greater emphasis on software optimization rather than hardware acquisition.

At the same time, NVIDIA and other chip manufacturers faced an urgent challenge. If they wanted to maintain their dominance, they needed to prove that high-end GPUs were still critical for AI breakthroughs. This might push them to invest more in AI software themselves, integrating better optimization techniques into their hardware offerings. Alternatively, they might need to develop new types of AI accelerators that cater to the efficiency-focused approach demonstrated by DeepSeek.

For now, the market remains in flux. DeepSeek's breakthrough has introduced a new level of uncertainty, forcing investors and companies alike to rethink their assumptions about what drives AI progress. The idea that the future of AI belongs only to those with the deepest pockets is no longer a given. The companies that adapt to this new reality—whether they are AI developers or chip manufacturers—will be the ones that define the next era of artificial intelligence.

The shockwaves from DeepSeek's breakthrough were not limited to the stock market. Almost overnight, the foundation on which the biggest AI companies had built their dominance was shaken, forcing OpenAI, Google, Microsoft, and Meta into a moment of reckoning. For years, these tech giants had operated under the assumption that artificial intelligence development required enormous computational resources, billion-dollar research budgets, and access to the most advanced chips in the world. But DeepSeek's achievement raised a question they weren't prepared to answer—had they been overinvesting all along?

The reaction within these companies was swift, and behind closed doors, there was a growing sense of unease. OpenAI, which had built its reputation as the undisputed leader in AI research, suddenly found itself in unfamiliar territory. It had poured billions into developing its latest models, forming deep partnerships with Microsoft to secure access to cutting-edge computing infrastructure. The idea that a startup with a fraction of its budget had developed a model that could compete with GPT-4-level performance was not just disruptive—it was a direct threat to OpenAI's business model.

Microsoft, as OpenAI's biggest financial backer, had a lot at stake as well. The company had invested tens of billions into OpenAI, integrating its models into core products like Bing, Azure, and Office. If AI development could be done efficiently at a fraction of the cost, then Microsoft's long-term strategy of monopolizing AI infrastructure through high-end computing resources might need to be reconsidered.

Google and Meta faced a similar dilemma. Google's AI division had been one of the most resource-intensive in the world, leveraging its proprietary tensor processing units (TPUs) and vast datasets to maintain a competitive edge. Its AI-powered search capabilities, Google Bard, and its cloud AI services all depended on the idea that the best models required massive infrastructure. Meta, too, had spent years building up its AI division, open-sourcing the LLaMA models while simultaneously investing heavily in AI research to improve its recommendation engines, advertising algorithms, and future AI-driven products.

The arrival of Janus Pro forced these companies into a difficult position. If DeepSeek's efficiency-focused approach was scalable, it could lead to a shift in AI development strategies, one that didn't require the kind of massive computing budgets they had built their businesses around. It meant that smaller companies, startups, and even independent researchers might be able to train competitive AI models without needing access to billion-dollar supercomputers.

Sam Altman, OpenAI's CEO, was one of the first to respond publicly. His reaction was both dismissive and defiant. Rather than acknowledging DeepSeek's efficiency as a potential game-changer, he doubled down on OpenAI's approach, stating bluntly that OpenAI would simply release better models. His message was clear—OpenAI wasn't worried about DeepSeek's breakthrough because it planned to maintain its lead through continued investment in ever-larger AI systems.

But his words hinted at something deeper. By reaffirming OpenAI's commitment to scaling up its compute resources rather than embracing a more efficient approach, Altman signaled that OpenAI saw no alternative to its billion-dollar strategy. The implication was that OpenAI would continue along the same trajectory, relying on ever-more-powerful hardware, exclusive partnerships with Microsoft, and a near-limitless budget to ensure that its models stayed ahead of the competition.

This response, however, revealed a potential blind spot. If OpenAI was unwilling to adapt to the new reality that DeepSeek had exposed, it could find itself stuck in an unsustainable arms race—one that may not be necessary for AI development to continue advancing. While DeepSeek had proven that a leaner approach could work, OpenAI and its backers were effectively saying that they would keep pushing forward with brute-force methods, regardless of cost.

Within the AI community, this stance drew mixed reactions. Some saw it as a sign of confidence, a way for OpenAI to reaffirm its dominance and assure investors that it wasn't about to be outmaneuvered by a startup. Others, however, saw it as a refusal to acknowledge that AI research might be heading in a different direction. The tech industry had seen similar moments before—large companies resisting change in favor of maintaining the status quo, only to be forced to adapt later when new players disrupted the market.

Google and Meta, for their part, remained quieter in their public response, but internal reports suggested that both companies were watching DeepSeek closely. Google had long prided itself on being the leader in AI research, and the possibility that a company outside of Silicon Valley had figured out a way to challenge that leadership was unsettling. Meta, with its commitment to open-source AI, found itself in a unique position—on one hand, its LLaMA models had indirectly contributed to the rise of open AI development, but on the other, it was still operating within the same expensive infrastructure model as OpenAI and Google.

If anything, DeepSeek's success had introduced a new level of unpredictability into an industry that had, up until that point, seemed to be following a clear trajectory. OpenAI, Google, Microsoft, and Meta had built their AI empires on the assumption that progress required massive spending. DeepSeek had just proved that assumption wrong. Whether the tech giants would continue their path of escalating costs or start rethinking their approach remained to be seen. What was certain, however, was that the AI landscape had changed, and no one—not even the biggest players in the industry—could afford to ignore it.

Meta found itself in an unusual position as DeepSeek's breakthrough began reshaping the AI industry. Unlike OpenAI, which had aggressively pursued a closed, proprietary model, Meta had taken a different path by embracing open-source AI development. Its LLaMA models, first introduced in 2023, had been released with the goal of providing powerful AI tools to the research community. At the time, this was seen as a bold move, one that positioned Meta as a champion of open AI while also allowing it to influence the broader AI ecosystem. But when DeepSeek emerged as a serious competitor, Meta's leadership had to grapple with an uncomfortable possibility—had its own open-source philosophy inadvertently helped fuel the very disruption that was now threatening Silicon Valley's AI dominance?

There was a growing realization that DeepSeek had likely benefited from the advancements Meta had made in its LLaMA models. Since LLaMA's release, the open-source AI community had worked extensively on fine-tuning and optimizing the models, improving their efficiency and expanding their capabilities. It was entirely possible that DeepSeek had built Janus Pro by leveraging these collective improvements, refining them further with its own innovations in multimodal AI. While there was no direct evidence that Janus Pro was based on LLaMA, the timing of its development and the similarities in training efficiency suggested that DeepSeek had been able to accelerate its research by standing on the shoulders of open-source progress.

This created a dilemma for Meta. On one hand, it had long argued that open AI development was the right path forward, allowing for faster innovation and greater transparency. On the other hand, if DeepSeek had been able to build a powerful competitor using openly available research, it meant that Meta's strategy might not just be accelerating progress—it might also be enabling new rivals in ways it hadn't anticipated. The realization that a Chinese AI startup had possibly gained an advantage by leveraging open-source AI raised questions about how much control Meta actually had over the technology it was helping to shape.

Internally, there were discussions about whether Meta should reconsider its approach to open-source AI. While the company had benefited from being seen as a more transparent and community-driven alternative to OpenAI, there were concerns that its open-source philosophy might be eroding its competitive edge. If DeepSeek—or any other AI startup—could rapidly improve upon Meta's publicly available models and create competitive products, then what incentive did Meta have to continue sharing its research so freely? This was the kind of unintended consequence that few had predicted when Meta first embraced open-source AI.

Beyond Meta, the financial world was also beginning to reevaluate its assumptions about AI investment. For years, the dominant narrative in Silicon Valley had been that AI required massive spending—billions of dollars poured into data centers, high-end GPU clusters, and cutting-edge research teams. Investors had backed this vision enthusiastically, pouring funds into AI companies under the assumption that only those with the most resources could stay ahead. But DeepSeek's emergence had introduced a new element of uncertainty into this equation.

If an AI model could be developed at a fraction of the cost and still perform at a competitive level, then what did that mean for the future of AI investments? The companies that had spent billions building AI infrastructure now had to justify whether such spending was actually necessary. Venture capital firms and institutional investors, many of whom had been heavily backing AI startups based on their ability to secure massive computing power, began reassessing whether efficiency might be a more valuable metric than sheer scale.

This shift in thinking had immediate consequences. AI startups that had been raising funds based on promises of high-cost, high-performance AI now found themselves facing tougher questions from investors. If DeepSeek had been able to achieve so much with so little, then why were other AI companies demanding hundreds of millions in funding just to train a new model? The days of assuming that bigger budgets automatically led to better AI might be coming to an end.

At the same time, large tech firms faced a dilemma of their own. Companies like OpenAI, Google, Microsoft, and Meta had built their AI research divisions on the assumption that continuous investment in larger and more expensive models was the only way forward. But if DeepSeek's efficiency-driven approach proved sustainable, it could force them to rethink their spending strategies. Should they continue pouring billions into AI infrastructure, or should they start prioritizing research into more efficient training techniques?

This uncertainty was particularly evident in the stock market. While NVIDIA's dramatic loss of six hundred billion dollars in market value had been the most visible sign of investor anxiety, the broader AI sector was also feeling the effects. Companies that had positioned themselves as essential players in the AI boom saw their valuations fluctuate as investors weighed the possibility that AI development might not require the kind of hardware-intensive spending that had been assumed.

Even outside of AI, the ripple effects were being felt in related industries. Cloud computing companies that had been expecting long-term growth from AI workloads faced new questions about demand. Data center operators, which had been expanding rapidly to accommodate AI-driven computing needs, now had to consider whether a more efficient approach to AI could reduce the need for constant infrastructure expansion.

For years, AI development had been a race defined by who could spend the most. DeepSeek's emergence had disrupted that narrative, proving that intelligence and optimization could compete with brute force. The entire ecosystem—tech companies, investors, cloud providers, and hardware manufacturers—was now adjusting to a reality where efficiency mattered just as much as scale. What had once seemed like a straightforward competition to build the biggest and most expensive AI models had suddenly become far more complex.

Meta, along with the rest of Silicon Valley, now faced a crossroads. Should it continue embracing open-source AI, knowing that it might accelerate competition from unexpected places? Should tech giants rethink their spending strategies, recognizing that efficient AI development might be just as valuable as large-scale AI infrastructure? And most importantly, had the rules of AI dominance fundamentally changed?

As these questions loomed, one thing was certain—DeepSeek's breakthrough had permanently altered the trajectory of AI development. The companies that adapted to this new reality would survive. The ones that ignored it risked being left behind.

Chapter 5: The Political Battle – AI, China, and US Tech Dominance

Artificial intelligence has become one of the most contested battlegrounds in the ongoing tech rivalry between the United States and China. While trade wars and economic sanctions have long been a part of the geopolitical landscape, the AI arms race has introduced a new dimension to global competition—one that is not just about markets, but about the future of technological dominance itself. The ability to develop cutting-edge AI systems is now seen as a measure of national power, influencing everything from economic growth to military capabilities. And at the heart of this battle is the struggle over access to the advanced semiconductor chips that make AI breakthroughs possible.

For years, the United States has led in AI innovation, with companies like OpenAI, Google, Microsoft, and Meta at the forefront of research and development. This dominance has been reinforced by access to the most powerful hardware, particularly the high-performance graphics processing units (GPUs) and tensor processing units (TPUs) that are essential for training AI models. American companies, working closely with NVIDIA and other semiconductor manufacturers, have relied on these chips to power their AI models, and the U.S. government has recognized their strategic importance.

China, on the other hand, has been rapidly catching up. The Chinese government has invested heavily in artificial intelligence, making it a central pillar of its long-term economic and technological strategy. The country has fostered an ecosystem of AI companies—ranging from giants like Baidu, Tencent, and Alibaba to newer players like DeepSeek—focused on advancing machine learning, natural language processing, and computer vision. Chinese universities and research institutions have also made significant contributions to AI development, often working in parallel with corporate efforts.

However, the U.S. government has long been wary of China's rise in AI. One of the biggest concerns has been that advances in artificial intelligence could enhance China's military and surveillance capabilities, allowing it to build more sophisticated autonomous weapons, cyberwarfare tools, and large-scale data analysis systems. Washington has repeatedly framed AI as a critical national security issue, arguing that controlling the most powerful AI technology is essential for maintaining a strategic advantage over China.

In an effort to slow down China's AI progress, the U.S. government imposed strict export controls on advanced AI chips. The most significant of these restrictions targeted NVIDIA's high-performance GPUs, particularly the A100 and H100 models, which are widely used for training state-of-the-art AI systems. By preventing China from purchasing these chips, the U.S. sought to limit the country's ability to develop AI models that could rival those created in Silicon Valley.

The logic behind these restrictions was straightforward. Without access to the most advanced AI chips, Chinese companies would be forced to train their models on weaker, less efficient hardware, making it significantly harder to compete with U.S.-backed AI projects. Given the enormous computational demands of training large-scale AI models, even a slight disadvantage in chip performance could translate into delays or stagnation in research. The U.S. expected that by cutting off China's access to the best chips, it could slow down AI development and maintain an edge in the global AI race.

At first, these restrictions seemed effective. Many Chinese AI companies struggled to acquire the necessary computing power to train their models at the same scale as their Western counterparts. Some were forced to rely on stockpiled chips, while others explored alternative approaches, such as using cloud-based infrastructure located outside of China. The export bans also pushed China to accelerate its own semiconductor industry, with state-backed efforts to develop domestic alternatives to NVIDIA's chips. However, progress in this area has been slow, and Chinese-made AI chips have yet to reach the performance levels of their American counterparts.

But DeepSeek's breakthrough exposed a major flaw in the U.S. strategy. By developing Janus Pro using NVIDIA's H800 chips—a version of the H100 that had been designed to comply with export restrictions—DeepSeek demonstrated that high-end AI models could still be trained effectively, even without access to the most powerful GPUs. The fact that Janus Pro achieved GPT-4-level performance using hardware that was supposed to limit China's AI capabilities was a wake-up call for policymakers in Washington.

This raised an urgent question: if China could still produce competitive AI models despite chip restrictions, then were the U.S. sanctions truly working? If DeepSeek's efficiency-driven approach proved scalable, then it meant that the AI race was no longer just about who had the best hardware—it was about who could make the smartest use of the hardware they had. This realization posed a serious challenge to the U.S. containment strategy, suggesting that China's AI ambitions could continue advancing despite Washington's efforts to slow them down.

The success of Janus Pro also fueled concerns that China's AI industry might be more resilient than previously thought. While some Western analysts had assumed that chip shortages would significantly hinder China's AI research, DeepSeek's breakthrough suggested that Chinese firms were adapting quickly, developing innovative ways to bypass hardware limitations. This adaptability made it clear that while chip restrictions could still pose obstacles, they might not be the decisive factor in determining the outcome of the AI race.

Beyond the immediate implications for AI research, DeepSeek's success also had broader geopolitical ramifications. The U.S. and its allies had been debating whether to impose even stricter AI-related sanctions on China, including potential bans on cloud-based AI services that could allow Chinese firms to access foreign computing power. But with DeepSeek proving that efficient AI training techniques could work even with restricted chips, the effectiveness of such measures was now being questioned.

At the same time, China viewed DeepSeek's achievement as evidence that it could continue advancing in AI despite Western restrictions. If anything, the breakthrough reinforced China's determination to develop its own semiconductor industry, reducing its reliance on American technology. Chinese officials framed DeepSeek's success as a symbol of resilience, using it to argue that U.S. sanctions would not prevent the country from achieving its AI ambitions.

The broader AI war between the U.S. and China is far from over. While the U.S. still holds significant advantages in chip technology, cloud computing, and software development, China's ability to innovate under restrictions suggests that the competition will remain fierce. The lesson from DeepSeek's rise is that AI dominance is no longer just about access to the best hardware—it's about developing smarter, more efficient ways to train and deploy AI systems.

For the U.S., this means that simply restricting China's access to top-tier chips may not be enough to maintain an advantage. For China, it's a sign that AI breakthroughs can still be achieved despite external pressure. And for the rest of the world, it's a clear indicator that the AI landscape is shifting in ways that no one fully anticipated. The race for artificial intelligence supremacy is no longer just a question of who has the best technology—it's about who can adapt the fastest in an era of rapid change and geopolitical uncertainty.

When the United States imposed export restrictions on advanced AI chips, the goal was clear—limit China's ability to train cutting-edge artificial intelligence models and slow down its progress in the global AI race. The most significant part of these sanctions targeted NVIDIA's most powerful GPUs, specifically the A100 and H100 chips, which had become essential for training large AI models in Western tech companies like OpenAI, Google, and Meta. Without these high-performance chips, training massive neural networks at scale would become significantly harder, forcing Chinese AI companies to find alternatives.

At first, it seemed as if these restrictions were working. Many Chinese AI firms struggled to access the necessary hardware to train models at the same scale as their American counterparts. The sanctions effectively blocked them from acquiring the most advanced chips, creating a bottleneck that was expected to limit China's ability to develop state-of-the-art AI. But DeepSeek's breakthrough with Janus Pro showed that these restrictions were not as airtight as they appeared.

Instead of relying on banned hardware, DeepSeek trained its model using NVIDIA's H800 chips—an AI chip that was specifically designed to comply with U.S. export regulations. The H800 was a modified version of the H100, created as a workaround that allowed NVIDIA to continue selling to the Chinese market while staying within the legal boundaries set by Washington. Although the H800 was technically weaker than the H100 in certain aspects, it still provided a significant level of computational power, enough to support large-scale AI training when used efficiently.

DeepSeek didn't just work with what it had—it **optimized** its training process to ensure that it could get the maximum possible performance out of the H800 chips. Traditional AI training methods involve brute-force processing, where companies run massive amounts of data through high-powered GPUs over long periods. OpenAI, for example, used enormous clusters of H100 GPUs, consuming vast amounts of energy and computing power to refine models like GPT-4. DeepSeek, however, took a different approach.

By designing a more efficient training pipeline, DeepSeek was able to make up for the hardware limitations of the H800 chips. It used techniques such as model quantization, where lower-precision computations are used to reduce processing overhead, and adaptive learning rate scheduling, which optimizes how the model learns to ensure that every computation cycle contributes meaningfully to the training process. Instead of relying on excessive computational resources, DeepSeek focused on fine-tuning its data selection, ensuring that its model was trained on high-quality, highly relevant datasets rather than massive, unfiltered corpora.

This strategic approach allowed DeepSeek to train Janus Pro at a competitive level despite the supposed limitations of its hardware. While the

H800 chips were slightly slower and had reduced bandwidth compared to the H100, they were still powerful enough when used efficiently. DeepSeek's ability to maximize their potential proved that AI training was not just about access to the best chips—it was about how intelligently those chips were used.

The success of this strategy had major implications for the AI race between the U.S. and China. If DeepSeek could develop a model that rivaled GPT-4 while using restricted hardware, it suggested that China's AI progress might not be as dependent on high-end chips as U.S. policymakers had assumed. The belief that restricting access to top-tier GPUs would cripple China's AI development was now being questioned.

DeepSeek's ability to sidestep these restrictions also raised concerns in Washington about the effectiveness of AI sanctions. If companies could still train state-of-the-art models using legally available hardware, then future sanctions might need to be even more aggressive to truly limit China's AI capabilities. Some U.S. officials began discussing the possibility of expanding export controls further, potentially restricting not just hardware but also cloud-based AI training services that could allow Chinese firms to access computing power outside the country.

At the same time, China saw DeepSeek's success as proof that it could continue developing advanced AI despite external pressure. The breakthrough reinforced the country's push for semiconductor independence, accelerating government-backed efforts to develop domestic alternatives to NVIDIA's chips. While China's own chip manufacturing capabilities were still behind those of the U.S. and Taiwan, DeepSeek's achievement showed that even with existing limitations, Chinese AI companies could still compete at the highest level.

The geopolitical stakes of AI development had never been higher. By proving that it could work around U.S. restrictions without violating them, DeepSeek demonstrated that AI progress was not solely dependent on raw computational power. Instead, the key to advancing AI was developing more efficient training strategies—something that companies in both China and the West would now have to take seriously.

In the end, DeepSeek's approach to sidestepping chip restrictions was not just about surviving within a constrained environment—it was about redefining what was possible in AI training. By leveraging efficiency over brute force, it had challenged the fundamental assumptions of AI development, proving that innovation wasn't just about having the best hardware, but about knowing how to use it to its fullest potential.

DeepSeek's breakthrough in artificial intelligence didn't just send shockwaves through Silicon Valley and the stock market—it also caught the attention of the highest levels of government. The United States had spent years implementing policies designed to slow China's AI progress, relying on export controls to restrict access to the most advanced computing chips. But the revelation that a Chinese startup had managed to build a model rivaling GPT-4 using restricted hardware challenged the very foundation of that strategy. The White House was forced to respond, and President Trump made it clear that the United States could not afford to fall behind in AI.

In a public statement, Trump framed DeepSeek's rise as a wake-up call, urging American companies to accelerate their efforts and warning that AI dominance was a race the U.S. had to win. His comments echoed growing concerns among policymakers and industry leaders that artificial intelligence was no longer just a technological advancement—it was a matter of national security. He emphasized that maintaining leadership in AI was critical for both economic competitiveness and military strength, calling for increased investment in AI research and a stronger push to keep America at the forefront of innovation.

Trump's remarks signaled a potential shift in how the U.S. government might approach AI policy moving forward. Until now, the primary strategy had been focused on limiting China's access to critical AI technologies, particularly semiconductor chips from companies like NVIDIA. The assumption was that by controlling the supply of high-performance computing hardware, the U.S. could slow down China's AI capabilities and maintain its lead. But DeepSeek's success proved that China could still make significant advancements without access to top-tier chips, forcing Washington to reconsider its approach.

The White House's response was also a reflection of the broader debate surrounding AI dominance. For years, the U.S. had been seen as the uncontested leader in artificial intelligence, home to the world's most powerful AI labs and best-funded research institutions. OpenAI, Google DeepMind, Meta, and

Microsoft had built an ecosystem that attracted top talent from around the world, creating a near-monopoly on cutting-edge AI innovation. But China had been steadily catching up, with its government investing billions into AI research, developing its own language models, and integrating AI into industries ranging from finance to national security.

DeepSeek's emergence raised a fundamental question—was the balance of power in AI shifting?

The concern in Washington was not just about one Chinese AI model—it was about the broader implications of DeepSeek's approach. If a single startup could disrupt the global AI landscape with a more efficient training method, then China's entire AI sector could start moving in that direction. If more Chinese companies adopted efficiency-focused AI development, then U.S. restrictions on hardware might not be as effective as once thought.

For U.S. policymakers, the challenge now was figuring out how to respond. Some argued that the U.S. needed to double down on AI chip restrictions, tightening export controls even further to prevent companies like DeepSeek from accessing even modified versions of NVIDIA's chips. Others suggested that the U.S. should focus more on accelerating its own AI research, increasing government funding for AI initiatives and ensuring that American companies stayed ahead through innovation rather than restrictions.

There was also the question of AI openness versus secrecy. OpenAI had once championed the idea of open-source AI development, but as AI models became more powerful, it had shifted toward a closed, proprietary approach, keeping its most advanced models behind API access and corporate partnerships. DeepSeek, on the other hand, had taken an open-source stance, making Janus Pro's model weights publicly available. This raised concerns about whether the U.S. should reconsider its stance on open AI development—if AI research remained closed in the West but open in China, would that give China a long-term advantage?

The political debate extended beyond AI development itself and into economic and military strategy. AI was no longer just a tool for chatbots and content generation—it was becoming a critical factor in cybersecurity, autonomous systems, and defense applications. The U.S. had been working to integrate AI into military technology, from drone systems to intelligence gathering, and the idea that China was making major advancements in AI raised concerns about national security implications. If DeepSeek's efficiency-first approach allowed China to make rapid progress in AI-driven defense technology, it could undermine U.S. military superiority in future conflicts.

At the same time, there were economic implications to consider. The U.S. tech sector had benefited enormously from being at the forefront of AI, with companies like OpenAI and Google securing massive investments and partnerships based on their dominance in the field. If China's AI companies began gaining ground, Silicon Valley could lose its status as the world's undisputed AI hub, leading to shifts in investment patterns and capital flows.

The real question now was whether the U.S. could maintain its AI lead in the long run. Would the strategy of throwing more computing power and money at AI development continue to be effective? Or would DeepSeek's breakthrough force a rethinking of how AI research is conducted? If efficiency became the key to AI progress rather than brute-force spending, then the companies that adapted the fastest would be the ones that shaped the future.

For now, the U.S. remains the dominant force in artificial intelligence, but DeepSeek's rise has shown that dominance is not guaranteed. The AI race is no longer just about who has the best technology—it's about who can innovate the smartest, and that competition is far from over.

Chapter 6: The Open-Source Gamble – Will DeepSeek Win or Lose?

DeepSeek's decision to open-source Janus Pro was a bold move that set it apart from many of its competitors. In a time when major AI companies like OpenAI, Google, and Microsoft were increasingly shifting towards closed, proprietary models, DeepSeek took the opposite approach by making Janus Pro's model weights and code freely available. This decision had far-reaching implications, offering both significant advantages and potential risks.

One of the biggest advantages of open-sourcing Janus Pro was the opportunity for rapid community-driven innovation. By making the model publicly accessible, DeepSeek effectively invited AI researchers, developers, and enthusiasts around the world to fine-tune, modify, and improve it. The AI community had already proven its ability to enhance open-source models—projects like Stable Diffusion and Meta's LLaMA had seen rapid advancements as independent developers introduced optimizations, built specialized versions, and expanded their capabilities beyond what the original developers had envisioned. With Janus Pro, the same process could unfold, allowing the model to evolve in ways that DeepSeek alone might not have been able to achieve.

Another major advantage was the potential for wider accessibility. Many of the most advanced AI models are locked behind paywalls or API access, limiting who can use them and how they can be applied. By making Janus Pro open-source, DeepSeek ensured that anyone, from small startups to independent researchers, could access and build upon the technology. This could accelerate the development of new AI applications, particularly in regions and industries that may not have the financial resources to license expensive proprietary models from OpenAI or Google.

Open-sourcing also allowed for increased transparency and accountability. One of the biggest concerns in the AI industry is the potential for hidden biases, unethical applications, and opaque decision-making in proprietary models. By making Janus Pro open to the public, DeepSeek gave researchers the ability to inspect its architecture, understand how it works, and address any biases or vulnerabilities that might exist. This level of transparency was something that many AI experts had been demanding from companies like OpenAI and Google, which had increasingly restricted access to their models under the justification of safety concerns.

However, the decision to open-source Janus Pro also came with risks. The most immediate concern was the possibility that the model could be misused. While DeepSeek had likely intended for Janus Pro to be used for beneficial and ethical applications, making it publicly available meant that anyone—including bad actors—could take the model and modify it for unintended purposes. AI models have already been used to generate deepfakes, misinformation, and even malicious automation tools. Without safeguards in place, there was always the risk that Janus Pro could be exploited in ways that DeepSeek had not anticipated.

Another risk was that by open-sourcing its model, DeepSeek could lose control over how it was developed and deployed. Unlike proprietary AI companies that carefully manage updates, improvements, and commercial licensing, DeepSeek had effectively handed over its technology to the global AI community. This meant that multiple versions of Janus Pro could emerge, each tweaked and optimized by different developers. While this could lead to positive innovation, it also introduced the possibility of fragmentation, where different versions of the model developed in incompatible or even conflicting directions.

There was also the concern that DeepSeek's decision to open-source Janus Pro could inadvertently strengthen its competitors. OpenAI, Google, and other major AI players had access to vast resources, and nothing was stopping them from studying Janus Pro's architecture, learning from its design, and incorporating its best features into their own models. If Janus Pro contained innovative techniques or optimizations that could improve AI efficiency, there was a real possibility that competitors could extract those insights without contributing anything back to the open-source community.

Despite these risks, the open-source nature of Janus Pro created an unprecedented opportunity for the AI community to refine and enhance the model. Developers could fine-tune it for specific applications, such as medical diagnostics, scientific research, or advanced creative tools. Researchers could test new training techniques on it, optimizing its performance and expanding its capabilities beyond what DeepSeek had originally designed. Smaller AI labs could use it as a foundation for their own projects, reducing the need to start from scratch and accelerating innovation across the board.

The most significant potential lay in community-driven fine-tuning. With enough researchers and developers contributing improvements, Janus Pro could become more powerful over time, potentially rivaling or even surpassing proprietary models. The AI community had already demonstrated its ability to take open-source models and improve them—projects like fine-tuned versions of LLaMA had proven that independent developers could achieve results comparable to those of billion-dollar AI labs. If Janus Pro followed a similar trajectory, it could continue evolving far beyond its initial release.

In the end, DeepSeek's decision to open-source Janus Pro was a gamble—one that could either accelerate innovation or introduce new risks. Whether it would ultimately prove to be a strategic advantage or a vulnerability remained to be seen.

What was certain, however, was that by making Janus Pro freely available, DeepSeek had fundamentally altered the AI landscape, setting the stage for a new era of decentralized, community-driven AI development.

DeepSeek's decision to open-source Janus Pro was a bold move that invited both innovation and competition. By making the model freely available, it allowed researchers and developers around the world to refine and expand its capabilities. However, this openness also introduced a significant risk—competitors, including some of the biggest AI companies, could study Janus Pro's architecture, extract its best techniques, and use them to build even better models. In an industry where cutting-edge AI development is often a race to stay ahead, this was a gamble that could either accelerate DeepSeek's influence or undermine its own advantage.

The biggest concern was that companies like OpenAI, Google, and Meta—despite maintaining proprietary AI models—had the resources to analyze Janus Pro's design, learn from its optimizations, and integrate those insights into their next-generation systems. If DeepSeek had discovered a more efficient way to train AI using limited computational resources, there was nothing stopping larger companies from adopting similar techniques while still benefiting from their superior access to data, funding, and infrastructure. OpenAI, for example, had already established itself as a leader in AI research with deep pockets and vast computing power through its partnership with Microsoft. If it could incorporate the best aspects of Janus Pro into its own models while continuing to operate in a closed, tightly controlled environment, it could effectively leapfrog DeepSeek while keeping its innovations proprietary.

Another risk was that open-source AI development meant that multiple independent teams could experiment with Janus Pro, leading to variations that might outperform the original model. AI researchers around the world, particularly those specializing in model fine-tuning and optimization, had already demonstrated that they could take an existing open-source model and enhance its efficiency, accuracy, and scalability. The AI community had done this before with models like Meta's LLaMA, where independent developers quickly optimized and fine-tuned the base model, sometimes achieving performance levels that rivaled or even exceeded their original corporate-backed versions. If the same happened with Janus Pro, it was possible that an entirely new iteration of the model—built by an independent AI lab or startup—could emerge as a superior alternative, diminishing DeepSeek's influence in the process.

Beyond Silicon Valley, there was also the question of how other AI research hubs, particularly in China, might leverage Janus Pro's open-source foundation. The model's availability meant that competing Chinese AI companies could take its architecture, adapt it, and integrate it into their own projects without having to build from scratch. This could accelerate AI innovation across multiple firms, reducing DeepSeek's unique competitive edge within China's AI ecosystem. While DeepSeek had gained early recognition for its efficiency-first approach, it was now facing the possibility that other companies, using the very foundation it had created, could rapidly build upon its work and introduce even stronger multimodal AI models.

There was also the potential for non-traditional AI developers—companies outside of the usual big tech players—to capitalize on Janus Pro's open-source nature. Startups, academic institutions, and government-backed research labs could use the model as a foundation for their own AI advancements, potentially developing specialized versions tailored to industries like healthcare, finance, or cybersecurity. While this could lead to positive technological advancements, it also meant that DeepSeek would have little control over how its model evolved once it had been adapted by external parties.

The risk extended beyond competition—it also included the possibility that Janus Pro could be absorbed into larger, more powerful ecosystems. Tech giants with access to enterprise-scale AI infrastructure could take the open-source model and integrate it into their cloud platforms, making it available to businesses and developers while layering proprietary enhancements on top. This would allow them to offer Janus Pro-derived capabilities through subscription-based services while maintaining exclusive control over additional features, essentially using DeepSeek's own research as a stepping stone for their own business models.

Despite these risks, DeepSeek's open-source strategy was not without its potential long-term advantages. By inviting the global AI community to collaborate on Janus Pro, it positioned itself as a leader in a growing movement toward decentralized AI development. This could allow DeepSeek to remain at the center of future innovations, ensuring that its contributions remained relevant even as competitors built upon its work. Furthermore, by fostering a strong community of developers and researchers, DeepSeek could benefit from continuous improvements to its model without having to bear the full cost of research and development.

Ultimately, the question of whether open-sourcing Janus Pro would be a net gain or a competitive disadvantage remained unanswered. If DeepSeek was able to maintain leadership in the evolving AI landscape by continuously improving upon its own model, it could solidify its reputation as a pioneer in efficient AI development. However, if competitors—particularly those with greater resources—used Janus Pro as a foundation to build superior, proprietary models, DeepSeek risked losing its edge. The coming months and years would determine whether its gamble on open-source AI was a breakthrough strategy or a costly mistake in an industry that rewards those who stay ahead of the curve.

DeepSeek's decision to open-source Janus Pro stood in stark contrast to the increasingly closed approach taken by OpenAI and other leading AI firms. While OpenAI, Google, and Microsoft had moved toward tightly controlled, proprietary AI ecosystems, DeepSeek took the opposite path, releasing its model to the public and allowing independent developers to refine and expand upon it. This divide between open and closed AI development raises a fundamental question about the future of artificial intelligence—will open-source AI lead to more rapid innovation, or will it ultimately backfire by enabling competitors and bad actors?

OpenAI began as a nonprofit research organization committed to the idea of open and transparent AI development. When it was first founded, it published its research and models freely, believing that AI progress should benefit everyone. However, as artificial intelligence became more powerful, OpenAI shifted away from its original vision. With the development of GPT-3 and, later, GPT-4, OpenAI transitioned into a closed, for-profit structure. Access to its most advanced models was restricted behind API-based services, with OpenAI dictating how and where its AI could be used. The justification for this shift was twofold—first, concerns over AI safety and ethical misuse, and second, the need for sustainable funding to continue pushing AI research forward.

By contrast, DeepSeek took an entirely different approach with Janus Pro. Rather than monetizing access to its model, it made the weights publicly available, allowing anyone to download and experiment with the system. This decision aligned DeepSeek with a growing movement toward decentralized AI development, one that had been gaining momentum through projects like Meta's LLaMA and the open-source Stable Diffusion community. The philosophy behind open-source AI was that democratizing access to powerful AI models would accelerate progress, encourage transparency, and reduce reliance on a few dominant corporations controlling the technology.

The benefits of this approach were immediately clear. Open-source AI allowed for greater collaboration across industries, enabling developers, researchers, and startups to fine-tune models for specific applications without needing the massive resources of a company like OpenAI. This kind of decentralized innovation had already proven successful in other areas of technology, particularly in software development, where open-source projects like Linux had led to widespread industry adoption. If AI followed a similar path, open-source models could become the foundation for a new wave of AI-powered applications and services.

However, there were also significant risks associated with DeepSeek's approach. The most immediate concern was that by making Janus Pro freely available, DeepSeek had given up control over how its AI was used. While OpenAI could enforce strict usage policies and prevent its models from being deployed for harmful purposes, DeepSeek had no way to stop bad actors from taking Janus Pro and modifying it for unethical applications. This raised concerns about misinformation, automated cyber threats, and AI-generated content being used for malicious activities.

Another challenge was the potential for open-source AI to weaken DeepSeek's own competitive advantage. Unlike OpenAI, which retained full control over its proprietary models and could monetize them through partnerships and enterprise licensing, DeepSeek's open-source model meant that anyone—including competitors—could take its technology, improve upon it, and use it in their own commercial products. This had already been seen with Meta's LLaMA, where independent developers quickly fine-tuned the model and created versions that sometimes outperformed the original release. If Janus Pro followed the same trajectory, DeepSeek could find itself losing control over the very technology it had pioneered.

There was also the broader economic question of whether open-source AI could be sustainable in the long term. OpenAI had argued that training and maintaining large-scale AI models required enormous financial and computing resources, which meant that an entirely open approach was impractical. By restricting access to its models and securing funding from Microsoft, OpenAI ensured that it could continue developing more advanced AI systems. DeepSeek, on the other hand, had not yet outlined how it planned to sustain its AI research while keeping its models open-source. If it failed to secure long-term financial backing, there was a risk that it would be outpaced by competitors with deeper resources.

The debate over open-source versus closed AI was far from settled, and both approaches had their strengths and weaknesses. OpenAI's closed ecosystem ensured that AI models could be better controlled, secured, and monetized, allowing for continuous research and development. However, it also concentrated power in the hands of a few companies, raising concerns about monopolization and lack of transparency. DeepSeek's open-source model encouraged broader innovation and accessibility but introduced uncertainties about long-term sustainability, security risks, and potential loss of control.

The future of AI development may not be entirely one-sided. Some experts believe that a hybrid model could emerge, where companies release certain AI components as open-source while keeping the most powerful versions proprietary. This would allow for innovation while maintaining safeguards against misuse. Others argue that as AI becomes more advanced, governments may step in to regulate access, imposing new rules on whether AI models can be open-sourced at all.

What remains clear is that DeepSeek's decision to open-source Janus Pro has forced the industry to confront these questions sooner rather than later. Whether open-source AI becomes the dominant approach or ends up being a cautionary tale will depend on how well companies, researchers, and policymakers navigate the balance between innovation and security.

Chapter 7: What's Next? The Future of AI After DeepSeek

DeepSeek's success in developing a powerful AI model at a fraction of the cost traditionally required has sparked a major shift in how companies approach artificial intelligence. For years, AI development had been defined by an arms race in computing power, with major players like OpenAI, Google, and Microsoft pouring billions into data centers, GPU clusters, and proprietary research. But DeepSeek proved that with the right training techniques, AI models could achieve state-of-the-art performance without relying on brute-force spending. The question now is whether other startups will follow DeepSeek's lead or if Big Tech will double down on its existing strategy.

The implications of DeepSeek's breakthrough extend beyond one company's success. Startups, academic researchers, and independent AI labs are now watching closely, wondering if they, too, can build competitive AI models without the need for billion-dollar budgets. If cost-efficient AI development proves to be a scalable approach, it could unlock opportunities for smaller players to enter the field and compete with major tech giants.

Historically, the biggest barrier to entry in AI research has been access to computing power. Training models like GPT-4 required thousands of the most advanced GPUs running for weeks or months, a process that was prohibitively expensive for all but the largest companies. However, DeepSeek's ability to sidestep this requirement by optimizing training processes suggests that AI development may no longer be limited to those with the deepest pockets. This could lead to a wave of new AI startups focusing on efficiency rather than raw computational power, experimenting with alternative training methods that reduce hardware dependencies.

If more startups follow DeepSeek's lead, the AI industry could begin shifting toward a more decentralized model, where innovation is no longer concentrated in just a handful of well-funded companies. This could accelerate AI research in unexpected ways, as smaller teams with diverse approaches experiment with lightweight architectures, fine-tuning techniques, and optimized learning strategies.

However, while efficiency-based AI development presents exciting possibilities, it also raises questions about how Big Tech will respond. Companies like OpenAI and Google have spent years justifying their massive AI budgets, arguing that more computing power is necessary to push the boundaries of artificial intelligence. If cost-efficient models start closing the performance gap with proprietary ones, these companies may be forced to rethink their strategies.

One possible response is that Big Tech will simply spend even more. OpenAI, for example, has already signaled its intention to develop ever-larger models, with Sam Altman stating that OpenAI will release even more powerful AI systems in the future. If

OpenAI, Google, and Meta choose to maintain their dominance through sheer scale, they may invest even greater resources into training ultra-large models, hoping that size and raw computational power will continue to give them an edge.

On the other hand, some companies may decide to pivot toward optimizing their training methods rather than simply scaling up. If DeepSeek's success proves that AI models can achieve comparable performance with more efficient training, then Big Tech may begin shifting resources toward software-based optimizations, looking for ways to achieve better results with fewer computational demands. This could lead to greater emphasis on algorithmic efficiency, dataset selection, and adaptive training techniques rather than just increasing hardware capacity.

Another potential strategy for Big Tech is to integrate efficiency breakthroughs into their own closed ecosystems. OpenAI, for instance, could study DeepSeek's techniques and incorporate similar optimizations into its next-generation models while still keeping its models proprietary. Google, with its vast AI research division, may explore whether efficiency-based AI training can be used to reduce the costs of running its AI-powered services while maintaining high performance.

There's also the possibility that Big Tech will adopt a hybrid approach, balancing both large-scale AI development and efficiency-driven improvements. Companies may continue investing in ultra-powerful models for high-end enterprise applications while also supporting lightweight, cost-effective AI models for consumer-facing products. This could create a two-tier AI ecosystem, where some models are designed for mass accessibility and others remain locked behind expensive infrastructure.

Regardless of which direction the industry takes, DeepSeek's impact is undeniable. The company has forced the AI world to rethink the assumption that bigger is always better. Whether startups follow its example or Big Tech adapts by refining its approach, one thing is certain—the future of AI development will no longer be dictated solely by who has the most money to spend. The real competition will be between those who can innovate the smartest.

Janus Pro's open-source nature presents a unique opportunity for it to evolve beyond its original capabilities. Unlike proprietary models that rely solely on their creators for updates and improvements, Janus Pro is now in the hands of a global community of researchers, developers, and AI enthusiasts. This decentralized approach to AI development means that the model's potential is no longer limited by the resources of a single company. Instead, it can continuously improve as experts from different fields contribute refinements, optimizations, and new applications.

One of the most immediate ways Janus Pro can be enhanced is through fine-tuning. While the base model is already competitive with some of the best proprietary AI systems, independent researchers can train it on specialized datasets to improve its performance in specific areas. This could include medical research, legal analysis, scientific discovery, or creative fields like music and visual arts. By tailoring the model for niche applications, the AI community can create customized versions of Janus Pro that outperform general-purpose models in specialized domains.

Another major advantage of open-source AI is the ability to optimize efficiency. Developers can experiment with different training techniques, compression methods, and quantization strategies to make Janus Pro run faster and more effectively on a wider range of hardware. This could make the model more accessible to users with limited computing resources, potentially allowing it to run on consumer-grade devices rather than requiring high-end GPUs. If the AI community successfully optimizes Janus Pro to be lightweight while maintaining strong performance, it could challenge the dominance of closed-source models that demand vast amounts of computational power.

Beyond fine-tuning and optimization, open-source AI models often benefit from security and bias auditing. With Janus Pro's architecture available for public inspection, researchers can analyze its decision-making processes, identify biases, and implement corrections. This level of transparency is something that proprietary AI companies often struggle with, as their models remain closed to outside scrutiny. By allowing the broader AI community to review and improve its fairness, Janus Pro could become a benchmark for ethical AI development.

Community-driven enhancements could also expand Janus Pro's multimodal capabilities. While it already performs well in both text and image-based tasks, developers could integrate new functionalities, such as audio and video processing, advanced reasoning capabilities, or real-time interactions. By extending Janus Pro's abilities through modular updates, the model could evolve into a more powerful and versatile AI system than originally envisioned.

One of the most exciting possibilities is the emergence of collaborative research projects built around Janus Pro. Open-source AI communities have historically played a major role in advancing machine learning techniques, and with a strong enough network of contributors, Janus Pro could become the foundation for a new wave of AI research. Universities, independent labs, and AI hobbyists could work together to push the boundaries of what the model can do, leading to breakthroughs that might not have been possible within a single company's development pipeline.

However, the success of Janus Pro's open-source evolution will depend on how well the AI community organizes its contributions. While open-source models offer a high degree of flexibility, they can also suffer from fragmentation if different versions emerge without proper coordination. To maximize Janus Pro's potential, developers and researchers will need to establish shared goals, maintain transparency in their improvements, and create standardized benchmarks for evaluating updates.

If Janus Pro continues to gain traction within the AI research community, it could serve as a compelling alternative to the dominant closed-source models developed by OpenAI, Google, and Meta. With each iteration, as the model becomes more powerful, more efficient, and more specialized for different use cases, it could shift the balance of AI development away from centralized corporate control and toward a more decentralized, collaborative model.

Ultimately, Janus Pro's future is now in the hands of the global AI community. Whether it becomes a long-term competitor to proprietary AI models or simply serves as a stepping stone for new innovations will depend on how actively researchers, developers, and businesses engage with it. But one thing is clear—by making Janus Pro open-source, DeepSeek has set in motion a new chapter in AI evolution, one that could redefine how artificial intelligence is built, shared, and improved over time.

The open-sourcing of Janus Pro and DeepSeek's unexpected rise have introduced new questions about AI ethics, security, and regulation. As artificial intelligence becomes more powerful and widely accessible, concerns about how it is used—and who controls it—are more pressing than ever. Governments, businesses, and researchers are now grappling with the implications of open AI development and whether the balance of power in AI should shift away from centralized tech giants toward a more decentralized, community-driven model.

One of the most significant ethical concerns surrounding AI is the potential for misuse. Open-source models, while promoting transparency and innovation, also create opportunities for bad actors to modify and deploy AI in harmful ways. Misinformation, deepfakes, and automated cyber threats are just a few of the risks that emerge when powerful AI systems are freely available without safeguards. Unlike companies such as OpenAI and Google, which impose usage restrictions on their proprietary models, DeepSeek has relinquished control over how Janus Pro is used. This raises an urgent question—how can AI be kept safe and accountable when no single entity is responsible for overseeing its use?

Security is another critical issue. Open-source AI means that anyone with the technical knowledge can study, alter, and redeploy Janus Pro, including state actors, criminal organizations, or rogue developers. While openness can drive innovation, it also exposes vulnerabilities. Governments and regulatory bodies are already considering stricter controls on AI development, but enforcing meaningful oversight on decentralized AI models presents a unique challenge. If the most advanced

AI systems become freely available to the public, security risks could escalate beyond what current regulations can manage.

Regulatory responses to AI's rapid evolution have been fragmented and inconsistent. The European Union has led the way with the AI Act, aiming to impose strict guidelines on AI development, while the United States has taken a more flexible, industry-driven approach. China has implemented its own AI regulations, particularly in content moderation and censorship, but DeepSeek's rise suggests that even within regulatory constraints, innovation can thrive. The question now is whether global regulators will push for greater restrictions on open-source AI or find a way to support responsible AI development without stifling progress.

As AI ethics, security, and regulation remain in flux, the next chapter in AI innovation is unfolding. DeepSeek's success has demonstrated that disruptive breakthroughs no longer require billion-dollar budgets, and this could signal a shift toward a more competitive landscape where smaller players challenge the dominance of tech giants. If cost-efficient AI development proves to be a sustainable approach, more startups may emerge, each trying to push AI forward using smarter, more resource-conscious methods.

The implications of this shift extend beyond just AI research. If smaller AI firms can compete with Silicon Valley's largest corporations, it could change the way AI is commercialized and deployed. Instead of relying on a few dominant companies controlling access to AI, industries may begin to embrace a more decentralized model, where AI tools are built and maintained by a broader network of innovators. This could lower costs, increase accessibility, and drive faster improvements in AI-powered applications.

However, major tech companies are unlikely to let smaller players take the lead without a fight. OpenAI, Google, Microsoft, and Meta may double down on their current strategies, either by increasing spending to maintain their technological edge or by integrating more efficiency-driven approaches into their AI research. The competition between centralized and decentralized AI development could define the next decade of artificial intelligence, shaping everything from how AI models are trained to how they are used in everyday life.

Whether the future of AI belongs to smaller, more agile companies like DeepSeek or remains in the hands of a few dominant players remains to be seen. But one thing is clear—DeepSeek's breakthrough has changed the conversation. The assumption that only the biggest companies with the most expensive infrastructure can lead in AI has been challenged, and the industry must now adapt to a new reality where innovation isn't just about who has the most resources, but about who can use them the smartest.

Conclusion

DeepSeek's impact on the AI industry extends far beyond the release of Janus Pro. This is more than just the story of one AI model—it represents a fundamental shift in how artificial intelligence is developed, accessed, and controlled. For years, AI innovation was believed to be the exclusive domain of billion-dollar tech giants with access to the most advanced chips, the largest datasets, and the deepest financial resources. DeepSeek shattered that belief by proving that cost-efficient AI development could produce results that rivaled, and in some cases outperformed, the most expensive AI projects.

A six-million-dollar experiment was enough to make some of the biggest tech companies in the world rethink their entire approach to AI. The revelation that Janus Pro was trained on restricted NVIDIA H800 chips instead of the more powerful H100s forced Silicon Valley to confront an uncomfortable truth—bigger budgets and more compute power do not automatically guarantee dominance. OpenAI, Google, Microsoft, and Meta suddenly found themselves facing new questions from investors, the stock market, and even political leaders about whether their billion-dollar AI strategies were sustainable.

DeepSeek also exposed flaws in the U.S. government's AI containment strategy. The assumption that restricting China's access to high-performance chips would slow its AI progress now looks increasingly questionable. If DeepSeek could build a GPT-4-level model using limited computing resources, what else might be possible? The broader implications of this breakthrough are forcing Washington to reconsider its approach to AI competition, leading to debates over whether further restrictions are necessary or whether the U.S. needs to focus more on accelerating its own AI research.

The AI war is far from over. While DeepSeek has proven that innovation can come from unexpected places, OpenAI and other tech giants are unlikely to give up their lead easily. Some will respond by spending even more, betting that scaling up compute and data will continue to yield better AI models. Others may begin exploring efficiency-driven techniques of their own, refining training processes to reduce dependency on expensive hardware. Governments, meanwhile, are watching closely, as AI shifts from being just a technological advancement to a key factor in economic and military power.

The real question is whether DeepSeek's success will be a one-time phenomenon or the beginning of a larger trend. Will other AI startups follow its lead, proving that efficiency-focused AI development is not just possible but superior? Or will the dominance of big tech ultimately prevail, ensuring that the most powerful AI remains controlled by a few massive corporations?

The answer will define the next era of artificial intelligence. If DeepSeek's approach gains momentum, it could mark the start of a decentralization of AI development, making cutting-edge models more accessible to researchers, businesses, and individuals worldwide. If not, then AI may remain an industry where progress is dictated by those with the largest budgets and most computing power.

One thing is certain—DeepSeek has already left its mark. What happens next will determine whether its breakthrough was a disruption that forced big tech to adjust or the beginning of a revolution that changes AI forever.

www.ingramcontent.com/pod-product-compliance
Lightning Source LLC
LaVergne TN
LVHW022350060326
832902LV00022B/4353